had to escape to rest on "the other side of the lake," or sea.
On one occasion Jesus and His disciples had no leisure even to eat. So they climbed into a boat and

sailed for the lonely shore south of Bethsaida, the home of Peter, Andrew and Philip. Jesus often made use of the "little ships" belonging to the fishermen of the Sea of Galilee, which were propelled by oars and sails. He also used them as a pulpit from which He taught the crowds gathered on the shore.

But this time, He did not escape. The crowd had no intention of being left behind. They guessed where Jesus would take refuge and made the six-mile journey on foot to Bethsaida. When Jesus climbed out of the boat, thousands were already there, waiting for Him.

He did not rebuke them for their persistence. Nor did He plead that He was weary. He made them welcome, preached to them, and healed the sick.

It was April, a little before the feast of the Passover. The grass was new and tender green, starred

with small scarlet flowers. The days were warm and pleasant but when nighttime came it grew chilly.

After Jesus had been with the crowd all day, His disciples came to Him, rather worried. "This is a lonely place and the hour is now late," they said. They pointed towards the crowds of weary people. "Send them away, to go into the country and villages round about and buy themselves something to eat."

Jesus knew that by this time the crowd must indeed be hungry. It was the hour for the second meal of the day, which usually consisted of meat, cooked with rice, wheat or barley.

Whenever the Jews went on a journey, they carried a basket with them to hold their provisions. Since they had left their homes in haste to follow Jesus, their baskets were now empty of food and drink.

Perhaps to test them, because He knew what He was going to do, Jesus asked His disciples, "How are we to buy bread, so that these people may eat?" This puzzled them, especially Philip, who had charge of the money for the food supply which Jesus and his disciples shared together. "Two hundred denarii would not buy enough bread for each of them to get a little," he told Jesus.

Then Andrew, the brother of Peter, came to Jesus and said, "There is a lad here who has five barley loaves and two fish, but what are they among so many?"

Instead of answering Andrew, Jesus said, "Make the people sit down."

The disciples obeyed. They were used to dealing with the crowds. Quickly, they divided the men, women and children into groups of fifty and a hundred and made them sit down on the grassy hillside.

Jesus took the loaves into His hands and lifting His eyes to heaven, He blessed them. He blessed the fish in the same way. Then He gave the loaves and fish to His disciples to distribute among the people.

As each one took his share, the supply seemed to increase. To their amazement, five thousand persons received enough bread and fish to satisfy them, yet there was more than enough.

Jesus told His disciples, "Gather up the fragments left over, so that nothing may be lost." The disciples took baskets and, to their surprise, they were able to fill twelve baskets with bread and fish.

The people spoke to one another in awe. Their admiration for Jesus grew. They were deeply moved by His fatherly care and the way in which He had attended to their needs.

Both St. Mark and St. Matthew tell of another occasion when Jesus miraculously multiplied loaves to feed the crowd. The miracle took place not very far from where He had performed the first miracle. On the second occasion there were seven loaves of bread for 4000 people, and seven baskets of fragments were left over after they had all been fed.

In general, the Jews ate and drank in moderation. They began the day with a simple meal, carrying handfuls of olives, raisins, flat round loaves or goat's cheese to work, munching as they walked. When work was over, they ate their main meal, which they called "sitting at meat." They sat on mats or low seats around a table on which rested a central clay bowl, filled with meat and vegetables. This they scooped up with their fingers.

They made one exception to their moderate eating. At wedding feasts they enjoyed a great abundance of the richest food. There was meat, game, stuffed fish and other delicacies, strongly flavored with onion and washed down with wine. One of the kindest of Jesus' miracles was performed to save a host from embarrassment when the wine he had provided for the wedding feast ran out too soon.

Jesus and His disciples had been invited to a wedding in Cana of Galilee, a village about eight miles from Nazareth. He probably stayed with Nathanael, whose home was in Cana.

Depending upon the wealth of the family, a Jewish wedding lasted from three to eight days. The wedding to which Jesus was invited was an important one, presided over by a "steward of the feast," or master of ceremonies.

It was the custom for the bridegroom to bring his bride to her future home, having attendants carry her in a chair. The wedding procession was a happy one, with shouting, singing and dancing along the way. Bride and bridegroom were dressed in splendid clothes.

The marriage supper took place in the home of the husband's family and was a magnificent affair. The bridal couple sat under a canopy to receive their guests.

The family served the most extravagant meal that they could afford. According to etiquette, wine had to be served plentifully and it was a great disgrace if it ran out before the end of the feast.

Among the guests at the wedding feast in Cana was Mary, the mother of Jesus. To her dismay, she noticed that the wine pitchers were empty. Concerned for her host, she went quickly to Jesus and told Him, "They have no wine left."

Jesus said to her, "O woman, what have you to do with me? My hour has not yet come."

The use of the word "woman" in speaking to His mother may seem impolite to us. At that time, it was not so. In Aramaic, the language spoken by Jesus and Mary, "woman" was a term of the highest

courtesy. When Jesus said, "What have you to do with me?" He simply meant "Why do you bother about such things at this time?" He softened His remark by adding, "My time is not yet come." Jesus was not yet quite ready to use His miraculous powers.

But Mary felt quite sure that her Son would do as she asked. So she went quietly to the servants and

said to them, "Do whatever He tells you." At the entrance to the house stood six large stone water jars. Some were shaped like pitchers, some were two-handled. They were used to carry water to the house from wells, cisterns or streams. Each held twenty to thirty gallons and was used for storing water and for Jewish purification rites.
Jesus said to the servants, "Fill the jars with water."

The servants hastened to obey and were soon back, carrying pots of water on their shoulders or on their heads. They filled the stone water jars until they overflowed.

Then Jesus said, "Now draw some out, and take it to the steward of the feast." It was customary for the steward to taste the wine first, to make sure that it was good wine, ready to drink.

The steward tasted the wine and was puzzled. He called the bridegroom and said to him, "Every man serves the good wine first; and when men have drunk freely, then the poor wine; but you have kept the good wine until now."

This was the first miracle that Jesus performed. It has been called "the first, the kind miracle, when Christ joins in human happiness, happiness not sorrow." St. John puts this miracle at the beginning of his Gospel, considering it to be an important one. In His tender concern for man's needs, Jesus was ready to use His divine power to spare the bridegroom even a little embarrassment at his wedding feast.

After His death, when Jesus returned to earth, He visited His apostles in Galilee. Here again, He performed a miracle out of concern for man's needs.

Peter and Thomas, together with some of the other

apostles, had gone to the Sea of Galilee, the previous evening, to fish. They had fished all night but they had caught nothing.

When day dawned, they heard a voice calling to them from the shore. "Children, have you any fish?" They did not recognize that it was Jesus who was speaking to them.

"No," they said, discouraged.

Jesus said to them, "Cast the net on the right side of the boat and you will find some."

Perhaps they heard the note of authority in Jesus' voice, for they obeyed Him without question. And immediately the net was filled with fish and was so heavy that they could not pull it into the boat.

John was the first to realize that it was Jesus who had spoken to them. He said to Peter, "It is the Lord!" Peter, who was always impulsive, jumped into the sea, swimming eagerly towards his Master.

The other apostles followed him in the boat, dragging the net full of fish. They were only about a hundred yards from the land.

When they climbed out of the boat, they saw a charcoal fire burning on the beach. Jesus was standing near to it. "Bring some of the fish that you have just caught," He said.